the haiku year

the haiku year

Tom Gilroy
Anna Grace
Jim McKay
Douglas A. Martin
Grant Lee Phillips
Rick Roth
Michael Stipe

Soft Skull Press 1998

First Edition
April 1998

ISBN 1-887128-25-5

the haiku year was conceived and facilitated by Tom Gilroy with the help of Anna Grace.

Book design by Susan Mitchell

Soft Skull Editorial: Sander Hicks, Sparrow, Karla Zounek

Printed in the U.S.A. by United Graphics, an employee-owned corporation.

FOREWORD

Jim and I used to paint houses for Rick while we were students in Boston, about the same time we met Michael, around 1982. Rick would occasionally engage us in a "postcard challenge," where each participant had to send the others one classic '50s chrome card a day for, say, two weeks. During those challenges, each day had a beautiful little spin to it, like an extra cherry on a slice of cake or finding ten bucks in an old pair of pants.

Jim and I moved on to other cities and Michael started to tour a lot, and the postcard challenges somehow stumbled into haiku challenges. They were a shorthand way to stay in touch with where each others' heads were at, far more poetically and accurately than a four page letter could. In addition to the actual haiku, the entire missive itself carried important details: the match-book the poem was written on, or the smell of the torn hotel stationery, or the coffee stain, or the postmark, even the choice of stamps. It was all part of the thrill.

Fifteen years later, Jim, Michael, Grant and I were sitting with the lights off, listening to Clara Rockmore's beautiful Theremin CD, in Michael's hotel room in DC on a R.E.M/Grant Lee Buffalo tour. We made a pact to do a haiku challenge with each other (and Douglas, back in Athens, who later roped in Anna) for an entire year. To seal the deal we each wrote our inaugural haiku in pencil on the underside of the desk drawer in Michael's room. We were off.

Within a week the haiku year challenge was inspiring and changing what we noticed in our everyday lives. Suddenly each day seemed bejeweled, often at the oddest moments. The way the screen was ripped in a filthy gas station restroom suddenly mirrored some aspect of your life, and was beautiful. Or hilarious. Rick (who took up the challenge the second he heard about it) described it best, "It changed my life."

We were each supposed to write one haiku a day, but of course we all cheated once in a while. Even your guilt about the cheating taught you something about how you saw your life, your priorities, how you felt about poetry and your friends and how they felt about you. Any excuse for slacking was lame and inside we all knew it. Grant was the worst. Michael came next, then Jim, then Anna and me, then Doug and Rick. The days had extra cherries anyway.

Jack Kerouac and Michael McClure and the San Francisco Poetry Renaissance started the concept of Western haiku, which is what the haiku in this book are. Kerouac called them *pops*— little three-line poems aiming towards a kind of Zen Enlightenment. The Beat Generation was the right time to make a transition to a new kind of haiku, with all that pot-smoking and coffee-drinking and scatting everywhere and Japanese haiku books laying on couches next to Whitman and William Carlos Williams. A kind of combustion.

So they dubbed their haiku "Western" and chucked the 5-7-5 syllabic requirements of the three lines, but tried to stick to the thematic guidelines of the Japanese haiku as mastered by Bashō, Buson, and Issa, namely:

1. Seasonal references *(kigo)* to establish time and place.
2. The moment seized and rendered purely, captured in an instant of Buddhist (or Zen) enlightenment.
3. Reflections of the particular consciousness, or point of view of the author, his or her loneliness, or comedy, or anger.

We never intended for these to be published, they were just little gifts to one another across space. Hopefully you will accept these gifts with the love in which they were given. Take that love and go on to give your own most precious moments to the people you love. This book surely will have succeeded if mail carriers begin to notice an increase in postcards with three lines scribbled on them.

Then, slowly but surely the amount of poetry in the mail would increase, and cut in on the amount of junk mail we get. The evening news would have to start delivering a Poem of the Day instead of one more celebrity profile. People would have such a stockpile of precious moments they would no longer allow bombs to be made, wars to be declared, or people to walk around homeless or hungry.

The person who tells you this is impossible is the person you should start a haiku challenge with.

—*Tom Gilroy, October 1997*

THE FIRST FOUR
Washington, D.C.

MICHAEL STIPE

Ginger vodka
lavender tea
Life is good beyond this

GRANT LEE PHILLIPS

Leon Theremin's Ashes
Being blown from the speakers
sparks from a broken conductor

TOM GILROY

The radio landscape
colors the room
like fog

JIM MCKAY

Stale smoky sweatshirt
covers the lampshade
like a finished party

"Coffee and Pastry" sign
I thought it said "Poetry"
I would've ordered

under the floodlight
I see my breath
dissolve into the night

The midwest
is full of squares
from the plane

in the freezing phone booth
the wasp's nest
dangles unused

Try to make it new
so I fold the futon like
I saw in your house

hazy calculations
of what'll get me:
the bourbon or the cold tablets

Dark already?
I've barely been outside.
Winter.

Even "Amanda called"
on a scrap of paper
lightens my day

snow tires crush
red carnations
that fell off the hearse

Everyone I love
loves someone else, thinking me
too far away to love.

HAIKU.
gesundheit.

MS

the first step to a 12 stepper is
you are powerless?
what a load of shit.

MS

4

Tight shiny shoes
shift on clean carpet
uncomfortable squeak

Hood pulled tight
Shifting weight in the snow
Bus still won't come

the water froze in
the cat's bowl outside
a gold leaf contained in ice

the bedsheets in disarray
through a magnifying glass
antarctica

red nipple, naked buckle
goose bumps,
my skin, flint.

Broken thumb aches
Can't even button
My own fly

The black cat
in the white snow
monitors my movement

Your call woke me
but only adds
to my reverie

Bone-tired limbs
draped over shabby couch
wake up sore

Hotel bar back beat
Pulsing loud, music and smiles
Get me out of here

snow covered squares
on my mackinaw
like a heartland aerial view

the flapping plastic
covering the firewood
shatters the frozen night air.

he shivers from the cold
and the prospect of building
a future

downtown someone just
opened a sunglass hut
in the dead of winter

Bronners peppermint
dick. The shower's
hot. Gimmee.

Holding my baby's broken leg
we lie in the snow quietly
in agony

dogs frolic
in the snow
oblivious of the shovelers

Four guys on a flatbed
full of Christmas trees
unloading

The blizzard slows
Snow stops rushing
Begins to waltz.

Table for one
My eggs surrounded by
All last night's couples.

engine running, door ajar
she clips some holly
in the parking lot

Whitecaps on the Hudson
Seagulls struggle
Bobbing in flight

trying his glasses
on, myself i can't see
until i get closer

Holding in my pee
for an hour now—
I'm getting high

Robitussin
stopping my cough
rotting my teeth

giving up on you finally coming
i unplug
the christmas lights

middle of a blizzard
shoveling snow
will I ever learn?

Sunday paper pile
threatening the seduction
of this winter nap

Exhausted in a heap
I lie on the cold floor
Dreaming of work that ends

jingle jingle jingle jingle
bells. bang.
the salvation army blows over

Bitter cold wind
over damp ground
Old joints ache

White snowy sky
The seagulls are
Silhouettes.

Standing on the corner
lost in a missed phone call
unable to dig the snowfall

Amidst celebration
I'm thinking of war
Happy New Year

New Year's Day
confused,
a little sad.

1996
and punk rock just
makes me feel old.

with just my finger,
i wrote of our love
in the snow.

In the grip truck
I chew vitamin C
with the camera girl

Bright sun
through filthy windows
Shiny winter gloom

the drowned deer
wrecked on shore, her dark heart
glistens

cold-handed surprise
changing the lightbulb
encrusted with ladybugs

studied, drunk. youth
screams from your hairstyle.
it draws me, pulls me in.

Snowstorm dog
happier
than his owner.

before you could hang up
my machine caught
a half-second of bar-noise

getting older
a little worried about
running out of time

End of the pier—
January blizzard
the city's muted hum.

on the subway
the conductor calls your name
at every stop

Fighting
so hard
not to fight

hand under covers
in bed under sheets
sky outside of few stars

Gentleman?
Sensitive guy?
I wanna get fucked.

patio furniture
where we laughed
now covered in snow

conversation hearts
i eat them without even
reading the words

Jim draws a chalk heart
"Anna loves—??" he looks up.
Water spreads the heart out.

Threadbare sofa
Can't fix it
Can't throw it out

Desire pulls
stronger than
experience

a good parking place
the only thing he got
for valentine's day

Black cat
White snow
Tip toe

NATIONAL BASKETBALL ASSOCIATION

FRIDAY FEB. 4, 1972 — 8 P. M.

MUNICIPAL TAX $.25 — TICKET PRICE $4.00

COLONNADE $4.25

12	1	1
SECTION	ROW	SEAT

waiting with the flu
for the steam to fill
the bathroom

Outside
the scraping sound
of a single shoveler.

Walking away
Thought I heard you call me back
No such luck.

Nearly normal
i lapse
into apathy

Geography
separates us in body
and mind

A yolk broke
at my leap year diner breakfast
and I smiled.

In a parking lot
a boy dances with a lunch box
then, seeing me, stops.

Heavy drumbeat
Heavy bass and guitar
Cookie monster voice

not feeling that old
'til I see
the gray nose hair

dust balls
laundry pile
ambition

Words on a page
Distracting me
from what I want to say

she says this:
you should get out of your room
it seems more empty than full

What have we come to,
learning of one others' endeavors
in Daily Variety

Getting older
looking more
for the familiar

grey snow
melting to reveal
the garbage underneath

sleepblink. full moon.
she's breathing normal.
ok.

my picture
has been taken
down off his wall

my grandmother can't sleep either
she pours bourbon in two glasses
and fills the empty night

our bikes
locked up beside each other
circling elsewhere

heavy flow night
wind whipping the skylight
her tampon waits by the soap dish

No desire
to read the news—
my life's enough for now

Five dollar bill
Laying in the grass
Doesn't look green

Winter couples
in need of Spring
argue in the streets

feeling guilty thinking
something's wrong just because
her shower's long

freedom from paper
the ink like a cage
the bird returns to

clearing the truck
the branch snaps back
sprinkling pedestrians with raindrops

Sleeping in
Raining out
thanks

All through the subway car
boys showing off to
girls who are on to them

you're eight hours ahead
and I'm stuck watching
geraniums struggling in a desert

walk behind a boy
who walks like the boy
i ran away from

Outside the Nissan Auditorium
next to the Marlboro map
they kissed

practice nonviolence:
doing nothing is better
than feeding this drama.

the city falls behind
the Bay Bridge, the broad water
the fog filling my mind

Lonely rainy day
hoping to run into
someone I know

I bad dream you out
of my head with six
coffees and a phone call.

MS

The young couple
kisses furiously on the street
taunting America

End of March
waking to falling snow
has lost its charm

April first
winter's gonna fuck with us
for a few more weeks

punctual bluebird
scared in April
by a global warming blizzard

I know snow is beautiful
But I'm over it
Okay?

Torn condom wrappers
lying by the bedside
are no trouble to clean up

her eyes
like a dare
that falters

dryer buzz goes off
we're finished fucking
just as the towels are done

broken-potted lily
strewn on the pavement
of a rainy day

long walk in the rain
to find out i did not win
the lottery

rain-wet years of cuttings
sink underfoot
as he explains their eviction

black exhaust
rises to the 4th floor
meeting the geranium

deciding on a tape
I'm distracted
by the sparrows outside

Like these red berries
in the rain
I have no umbrella

Spring's envelope opens
the blue dusk blossoms—everything
seems possible.

despite the rain
the mother licks her hand
to wipe the child's face

In a grocery store
my sister's eyes laughing blue
under a parsley wig.

the first cardinal lands
as it's ringing
the second one while I'm on hold

fumbling with the padlock
i recall him
entering me

What do you mean,
gardening
is "in"?

The plaque reads:
"Six known deaths occurred here"
what a view

What do I do
with this love
that you don't want?

under
umbrella
find thee, quiver

Cool-ass soul-mate, yeah.
(heard through blankets of thick sleep)
yeah. cool ass soul mate.

your glasses left
without your face. sitting alone
on the windowsill

I'm listening to my voice
languid on a damp day
pull up the covers

A Love Supreme plays
through shitty speakers and
turns my ears to gold

How do I say
goodbye when you're not even
here to hear it

one question:
why should the sum of ecstasy
equal misery

grappa, witch hazel pads
lavender extract couldn't
mask the cologne on the phone.

Just one more beer
Hank Williams in my mind
gloriously sad

We used to sit around
and talk about doing something
at least

Wrecked, I remember
my calling card number
how pathetic

8

DECKER'S
HOLD'EM

HOLD 'EM
TRADE MARK
REG.
U.S. PAT. OFF.

**25
RINGS**

HOG RINGS

HOLD'EM

DECKER'S

HOLD 'EM

CLOSES SMALLEST TO LARGEST
ALL KINDS OF RINGS

LARGEST,
HEAVIEST, GUARANTEED
MALLEABLE IRON HOG
RINGER MADE WITH
HOLDING SPRING TO
GRIP RINGS.

Your design is ugly
and you're an asshole
"Can I help you?"

he supports the arts
in subtle ways like buying
books his friends borrow

billboard photos
of unbearable beauty and
sorrow, in b/w no words.

Quiet computer whir
Palpable anger
Modemed worldwide

a discarded quote, some
forgotten cause, found
with my name.

MS

My fingers
tracing your baby skin
forever

stacking chairs at closing
echo here
like everywhere else

walking Sunday morning
past all the churches
to quietly read Nin

front seat red truck,
father driving
and the son listens to a walkman

One beer leads to seven
I feel fuzzy
and old

early morning window blossoms
float by
like ticker tape

Young subway girls
stare at strollered babies
rapt and desiring

We trade hats, laughing
He smiles, says he loves some girl.
I take my hat back.

stoned
I'm sorry
the mind goes to love

I'm not going to
let you see me
sad. Chewable tabs.

MS

in this bar this girl
asks Hassan,
do you want to finger me

MS

Tang in a cup
a moment's pause at the counter
off to score valium

Expensive suit
What are you selling
Fucking moron

Killing the fly
I instantly felt
regret.

The Smiths on
Starbucks' sound system
another dream over

Fear
makes hate
makes fear

Rage loud in 4/4
Knock me down
Knock me out

I me mine myself
Listen
Just fucking listen

Pristine apartment.
Fresh bird-shit on the armchair.
The window open.

"the sunflower don't care
on its first day
it's raining"

First hot day
and my stomach's still
in winter

checking out the miniskirt
I almost missed
Robert Frank walking by

at the foot
of the Miamisburg burial mound
the sons of Columbus tee off

F-train girls
completely aware
of their girlhood

Vital truths
protected by clergy
dead as a doornail

Soy Cuba memory
Light miracle in a dark room
Kino eye heaven

Man stutters bank talk,
a drunk beetle on pink tile,
fat belly, skinny limbs.

I stand mute
She reads the paper
and doesn't look up

The grown man
encourages the gardening woman
"Squirt the cat, squirt the cat!"

stand on the fire escape,
a bird comes. "Hey buddy" I say.
he stays.

median wildflower project
it's a wonder these people didn't
just give up long ago.

walking, rains come down.
we run for cover, dad and me,
and watch the rains change.

delicate air
luminous tree, dusk light
why go inside?

A weak cup of coffee
sets the tone
for a bad, rainy day

No fried eggs or grits
and despite your rising loudness
The French cannot understand English

Feeling the weight
on subway mothers
corralling their children

automated sprinklers mist
over lawn
the rain just drenched

Wondering
if I could marry
this girl on the train

Feet touching
legs brushing
hearts beating

your list of things
to do. my name
glaringly absent

two apple seeds
on a green felt table,
his pajamas

If AIDS was NASA
we could dump in millions, tune in,
and thrill to our advancements in fixing it.

From the plane
a thousand clouds
cast island shadows

BOBCATS

SAN MARCOS, TEXAS

That red lipstick
is the stuff of dreams,
not kisses.

I try to forget:
Home at 12:30, you called at
12:15. The red light blinks.

friendly machinations
just a dithering distraction
so fuck being nice

woke up to piss
found geranium clippings
in the bowl

on the bicycle
i rack myself
trying to take off too fast

kid consciously slowing
to help grandma carry
her tray of impatiens

Saturday night
Falling in love
with another bartender.

Ferns he pulled
for transplanting
dead on the picnic bench

Art arrives
Flat and uninspired
Lazy bastard

Pavarotti
the sorrow of war
in your tenor

Bosnia
I missed you
I'm sorry

i have a hard time
throwing away
even the plain carbon copies

Talking to himself
he makes me feel at home
in this Starbucks

Glasses and a book
left on the table
Juan dragged off and murdered

Midwesterners
intimidated by
ten variations of coffee

in his jaguar
he takes me
to my biology final

the iced coffee dripped
on the envelope piece
making it a better bookmark

he enjoys the sun
like a lizard or
some rare element he is

roof painted silver
red clouds nuclear rays boiling surreal
over manhattan

under the lemon tree
the fresh smell, the bright yellow
his face so close, it blurs

Return to Brooklyn
Water drips from an AC
my room filled with lost sun

That crew-cut boy,
fourteen, shirtless, Polish, punk,
looking at me looking.

smell of gasoline parking lot.
covers up the
scent of freshly dried blood

home so late
the street's empty. 2 stray dogs
stock still, staring.

my slab got poured
and we're having a
shin splint party

want to just go
naked. no clothes
not even a watch

you didn't know
you liked it
'til I did it

There's thunder outside
up on the roof the wind blows
across the sky

These desert rocks, beautiful
like you, love
can shift at any moment

The coyote
is a wacked-out brother
always doing wrong

The map on my bed
unfolded, blue, green, alone.
Look, these roads go to you

The desert rains.
The dogs are wet, sleeping outside.
The old house crumbles.

Walking the streets
looking for love
from perfect strangers

A Hupmobile, where
couples paid a quarter to
sit under that tree.

ms

the water in front
darkens as the wave behind
approaches

the sun, green
refracted through a wave
right before it hits me

old couple floating
over the waves at sunset
the bullshit way behind them

the littlest ant in
the world
navigates my page

MS

precipitation
happens slowly, like the ketchup ad,
your body with mine

City full of rain.
Not raining, just wanting to.
It's so hot. You have to wait.

the tinkle of the glass
in the sweating iced coffee
like Dad in '66

Phone rings loudly
Machine begins clicking
I sit

blue smoke comes in my window
from the Dads
testing firecrackers

Selling preppy golf shirts
so rich people can find each other
and breed

smashed
that fucking mosquito
guess I'm no Buddha

the coffee was driving—
what did I sputter
when I called.

ms

Black eye, swollen hand
Macho silence festering
Blown gasket, sad life

Old love letters
Read quickly
and thrown out

Even in this antiseptic AC
I close my eyes
and smell your skin

permiso, pero it's gross
a seashell
as an ashtray

deafening cicadas
immobile iguana
but the surf still sounds like traffic

coffee grounds, banana
peels, tin cans. half a grapefruit;
cartoon garbage.

ms

feeling weird
smelling charcoal briquets
but not chlorine

Billy got a kiddie pool
keeps it on the roof
now I'm a fish at sunset

blood showing, shirt wet
my tire goes flat, legs on fire
I walk through green rain

Bitter stamp taste
Licked for a letter
that will get no reply

politics aside
the sunset loses a little
without her here

NON-OFFICIAL
FUN TARGET

#NFT-3

Moose

NAME_____
SCORE_____

In that Summer
near-dark moment
when the street lights come on

I'm twixt between the
two of you. who has the
smaller house. I've been to both.

Freshly shaved
Freshly showered
Bill lies dead four days

(still life)
of acupuncture and eyeshadow
plant life and German chocolate carpet
talking teeth and the planets

bleak lights flare.
the train rolls past
open stars

crickets caress
in the pause between
turning out the light and reaching the bed

she scoops the popcorn
off her palm
with her tongue

milk drips, a big balloon, tied
to your wrist. pawpaw
eats jalapeño peppers.

Young father
ashamed and at a loss
with his baby girl

the drunken wasp
orange like candy, climbs
and falls, and climbs again.

Between wet reeds and tall trees
a man walks. The city's lake
filled his bag with fish.

a subway platform
waiting. the buzz warns "train-train"
we stand up to wait.

Your grandma's dead
I ask what to feel
I never liked her

late afternoon bug repellent
and Ssssting Stop
is my perfume.

MS

Fat train switchman
claps donut sugar from hands
unaware of the office laughter

PA-134 One of the 7 Tunnels on Pennsylvania Turnpike Between Pittsburgh and Harrisburg, Pa.

In a cold sweat
I wake and remember
which way a razor cuts

know we're in
Tennessee once the restroom
walls start to alienate

While you talk
about yourself
I'll daydream

the test:
how to face the day
how to spit in its eye

Mid-afternoon subway
dust-covered guys in work boots
going home.

awnings, neon, weird sun,
parking lots, smell, mist.
I'm coasting Memphis.

MS

Grey and dull red
Squirrel corpse
along 45 feet of blacktop

Subway smell
stuck in my nose
and driving me crazy

wondering as it sizzles
how many times I've put out
the joint in a drop of coffee

Pizza and cardboard
smells like my
New Jersey childhood

Short guy drives up
Confederate flag behind the cab
still short, he drives away

The crowd
on the sidewalk
waiting for leadership

Norton anthology
Men writing haiku about panties
Pisses Linda off

Old LSD tales
excite stale neuron jumbles
into clairvoyancy

horoscope says
vulnerability to love
no fuck

mistaking this loneliness
for hunger i want
to cry out starving

Haiku motherfucker
Burning spiritual jag
Enlighten my ass

green tin poor box
nailed to a post
below christ's feet

Japanese businessman
stares at her ass and says "sexy"
international asshole

You introduce me.
She almost hugs me, but smiles.
A smile through her from you.

The pizza box
warms my thighs
on the drive home

Little boy
confused
by his Sunday father

In the yellow light
of the bathroom mirror
black and blue looks green

dressed like gangstas
kids fish in
summer's last breath

Girl at the market
where I buy fruit, smiling
when I come to her stand

geese overhead;
the radiators'll be
tapping soon

stuck me, window-lost;
a squirrel jumps
from one tree to the other

without wind
you don't smell the chamomile
until you pull it up

looking at the moon
trying to figure
the rhythm of the ceiling fan click

A broken chair
Unpainted storm windows
Let's go fishing

since she's gone
the sheets only
smell like bleach

left outside in the rain
even plastic flowers
fade.

MS

Eighteen hours of work
and no money
ah, sweet bed

Bulging veins and sweat
Guitar blasts and venom
Iggy rules

Smoke on my jacket
Beer on my shoes
Was last night fun?

Checking my service
every ten minutes
modern life outta hand

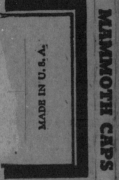

EXTRA LOUD

MAMMOTH CAPS

MAMMOTH CAPS

MADE IN U. S. A.

People in cars
telling life stories
in red light glances

Kerouac! Cassady! Bashō!
In the airport bookstore!
I forgot where I'm going.

Just for a moment
Jim walks and I see Michael
his friend inside him

hitching at autumnight
the red house's porchlight
flickers once

Alone
in a crowded bar
not belonging

ritalin slow down, M&M's
speed up. 1984 born.
channel surf standard.

MS

moonlit pumpkins
make the compost-walk
worth it

Your sultry voice
and wry smile
are affecting my hips

the father pushing
the kid on the tricycle
when it's easier to tell him to pedal

phone rings
crow calls
I fear bad news

Sex at night
Sex in the morning
Shit-eating grin

I'd sooner chew off my leg
than get trapped
in that city.

MS

Blue eyes, a smile
Swinging hips
In love for a minute

the path divides
the collapsed barn
from the torched garage

the chill air has taken
the ginger lily smell.
backup summer.

hiking up her miniskirt
she thinks I'm looking at her legs
but is ok with it

Pumpkin beer
it's good! the yard of leaves
the fall smiling at us

Psychedelic girls
with guitars
It's a wonderful world

Nana's voice
cracks and strains
alone in a big chair

fallen down bike
still locked to the rack
during football practice

old man
faking a phone call
to check the coin return

Sitting alone
with wine and spaghetti
I crack myself up

Whitney tourist listens
to his guided tour headphones
and walks by Ginsberg

soiled. wet. smiling.
the baby picture
sticks to the sidewalk

F Train triangle
of newspapers—
Spanish, Russian, Chinese

Drunk man asks what I drink
and can he please buy one for me
I say no and then can't take it back.

empty High School
field at dusk
the cord snapping the flagpole

Taking out Brooklyn trash
I think of Georgia
and friends' compost piles

Singing opera
he hands out porn fliers
on upper Broadway

driving & dreaming you in Arizona
STRONG CROSSWINDS POSSIBLE
between two buttes

boy with a hickey
on his neck that matches
the ink spot on his shorts

film executive girl
has a bleeding ulcer and a freezer
full of frozen pudding

the dishwasher clicks off;
time
for the news

A love so deep, ends
with a kick in the head
and the door locked

Pizza in a box
Coke in a can
Big fat life

Nana apologizes
"The house is so dirty"
It's clean

earthworm jim vs. the tick
the bus throws a little action
into snickers overdrive

White-hatted frat boys
Standing in a herd
Fucking clueless

Hot roasted turkey
gravy and all the trimmings
It's still a bird

Environmental my ass
full of false claims
I'll compost your ads

waking in an empty house
with a bathroom clinging
to perfume and steam

I sit stone-faced
Your sobbing
Just pisses me off

Rows of great books
I grab Rolling Stone
and feel like shit

Rush hour train
It's all sports pages
and bad cologne

these dust-bunnies spoil
the serenity
of the dump I'm taking

All the kids
want to wear advertisements
This country's fucked

Driving past
the arguing couple
feeling helpless.

800,000 Indonesian murders
1965 CIA-aided bloodbath
I need a face

MISSION VIEJO ELKS

•

25092 MARGUERITE PKWY.
MISSION VIEJO, CA
92692
#830-ELKS

FOR SAFETY STRIKE ON BACK

ELEVEN O'CLOCK TOAST

My brothers, you have heard the tolling of eleven strokes. This is to impress upon you that with us the hour of eleven has a tender significance. Wherever an Elk may roam, whatever his lot in life may be, when this hour falls upon the dial of night, the great heart of Elkdom swells and throbs. It is the golden hour of recollection, the homecoming of those who wander, the mystic roll call of those who will come no more. Living or dead, an Elk is never forgotten, never forsaken. Morning and noon may pass him by, the light of day may sink heedlessly in the west, but ere the shadows of midnight shall fall, the chimes of memory will be pealing forth the friendly message, "To our absent brothers."

how many more times will I
use the to-go bag
as a placemat?

Head buried in a book
She looks up
Smile full of braces

i would like
to take that CAUTION ribbon
and wrap it around my neck

[Big Gulp]
thou shall not partake
of the foods so great
as to challenge the mouth

I'm an easy cry on
planes; People Magazine, quintets
burn victim, Down's syndrome.

MS

Trying to be positive
But this bad performance art
is testing me

Suspicious parents—
I'm just smiling at your kid
Fuck this shitty world

she made this soup
that made me brrrp for hours   MS
fart puppy breath.

Dining alone
the man laughs
at his fortune

you cruise girls for me
"we'll never meet another us"
you say, still looking.

something rustling
in the skunk cabbage
as I slip in the swamp

Air and light
Time without action
Sunday afternoon dreams

everything's golden
when we kiss
behind my eyes

hauling wood
with my father
sound of wings

drunk;
this shithole;
I am indigenous

At the light
she lets me go
we both smile

caught by the curtain-wind
this morning I feel her
in another city

at dawn
we fall asleep
mid-sentence

early snowfall
vestibule wondering
will this old shovel go one more?

this refrain of you
returns, returns, returning again
without end

ご 伝 言
MESSAGE

Hotel Okura
TOKYO

Tom Gilroy (TG) is an actor, director, and playwright from New York. He is the co-founder (with Lili Taylor and Michael Imperioli) of the theatre company MACHINE FULL, for which he has written and mounted over a dozen pieces. He has appeared in several films, including *Land & Freedom*, *Girls Town*, and *Ratchet*, and is the director of the internationally acclaimed short film *Touch Base*.

Anna Grace (AG) is a writer and performer who lives in New York. She co-wrote and appeared in the movie *Girls Town*, winner of two awards at the 1996 Sundance Festival. In 1997, she received a fellowship from The MacDowell Colony.

Jim McKay (JM) is a film and videomaker and co-founder of C-Hundred Film Corp. He co-wrote and directed *Girls Town*, his first feature film.

Douglas A. Martin (DM) is the author of two poetry collections, *my gradual demise & honeysuckle* and *Servicing the Salamander*, as well as a novel as yet unpublished.

Grant Lee Phillips (GP) is best known as a songwriter and a recording artist. Under the title of his musical group Grant Lee Buffalo, he has released three critically acclaimed albums to date with a new one in the works. Venturing into other forms of expression such as the haiku is in keeping with his nature. Phillips is also fluent in the visual arts.

Rick "Biskit" Roth (RR) has been a hardcore human rights actvist for almost twenty years, coordinating a dedicated group of Amnesty International volunteers in Somerville, Massachusetts. He is owner of Mirror Image, an award-winning screenprinting shop, known for their fine art reproductions on T-shirts. He is the proud father of four daughters.

Michael Stipe (MS) is a singer/songwriter, photographer, and film producer. This is his first inclusion in a publication of haiku.

Your Haiku

Visit the interactive haiku machine: www.mirrorimage.com/haiku

Index

Soft Skull Press
50 E. 3rd St. #5A • NYC • 10003

The Kentucky Rules

by Cynthia Nelson
with illustrations by Tara Jane O'Neil
Available June 8, 1998

Indie-rock sensations Cynthia Nelson and Tara Jane O'Neil
return to press with a second collaboration in poetry and art,
following their acclaimed Soft Skull collection *Raven Days*. With
their band Retsin and books like *The Kentucky Rules*, Cynthia
and Tara have created a body of work that supports an earthy,
direct, self-possessed vision.

REPUBLICAN LIKE ME:
A Diary of My Presidential Campaign

by Sparrow
Available now

"All slaves freed, all debt forgiven" was his campaign promise.
He unveiled shocking proof that Lincoln was a Marxist. How
could Sparrow NOT have beaten Dole for the GOP nomination?
Find out in *Republican Like Me,* the story of the vociferous and
impassioned campaign trail of a revolutionary poet.

"One of the funniest men in Manhattan....Over and above
everything else, Sparrow offers something to believe in."

Robert Christgau
Village Voice

Distributed to the trade by Consortium Book Sales & Distribution, 1-800-283-3572
Access www.softskull.com for the latest Soft Skull catalog, text, and information.